SPORTING CHAMPIONSHIPS
WORLD CUP

David Whitfield

WEIGL PUBLISHERS INC.

Published by Weigl Publishers Inc.
350 5th Avenue, Suite 3304, PMB 6G
New York, NY 10118-0069

Website: www.weigl.com

Library of Congress Cataloging-in-Publication Data

Whitfield, David.
  World Cup / David Whitfield.
     p. cm. -- (Sporting championships)
  Includes index.
  ISBN 978-1-59036-695-0 (hard cover : alk. paper) -- ISBN 978-1-59036-696-7 (soft cover : alk. paper)
  1. World Cup (Soccer)--History--Juvenile literature. 2. Soccer--Juvenile literature. I. Title.
  GV943.49.W48 2008
  796.334--dc22

                              2007012105

Printed in the United States of America
1 2 3 4 5 6 7 8 9 0 11 10 09 08 07

Project Coordinator
James Duplacey

Design
Terry Paulhus

All of the Internet URLs given in the book were valid at the time of publication. However, due to the dynamic nature of the Internet, some addresses may have changed, or sites may have ceased to exist since publication. While the author and publisher regret any inconvenience this may cause readers, no responsibility for any such changes can be accepted by either the author or the publisher.

Every reasonable effort has been made to trace ownership and to obtain permission to reprint copyright material. The publishers would be pleased to have any errors or omissions brought to their attention so that they may be corrected in subsequent printings.

Further Research

Many books and websites provide information on the World Cup of soccer. To learn more about the tournament, borrow books from the library, or surf the Internet.

Books to Read

Most libraries have computers that connect to a database for researching information. If you input a key word, you will be provided with a list of books in the library that contain information on that topic. Non-fiction books are arranged numerically, using their call number. Fiction books are organized alphabetically by the author's last name.

Online Sites

FIFA's website, **www.fifa.com**, contains information about the history, rules, background, and events related to soccer for men and women.

The official United States Soccer site, **www.ussoccer.com**, has information about the game, including its history, statistics, and rules.

The International Football Hall of Fame, at **www.ifhof.com**, has information and facts about the world's greatest players.

Background information on every World Cup that has been played can be found at **www.planetworldcup.com**.

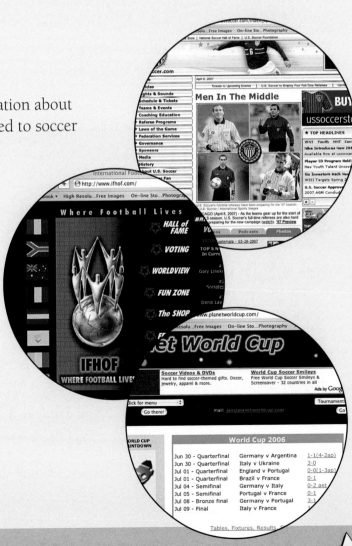

Glossary

bye: going to the next round of a series or competition without having to play an opponent or a qualifying game

coordination: the ability to use different parts of the body together smoothly and efficiently

cleats: spikes on the bottom of athletic shoes that give a player better traction on the field

end line: line running across the back of the playing field that marks the out of bounds boundary

golden goal: goal scored in extra time that wins the game

hand ball: intentionally handling, striking, or propelling the ball by a player other than a goalkeeper

round-robin: a tournament in which each competitior plays the others

shootout: a series of penalty kicks that decide the winner of a game that is tied after regulation time and overtime

side line: line running down the side of a playing field that marks the out of bounds boundary

tournament: a series of games between a number of competitors

World War I: war that lasted from 1914 to 1918 and included the continents of Asia, Australia, Europe, and North America

World War II: war that lasted from 1939 to 1945 and included the continents of Asia, Africa, Australia, Europe, North America, and South America

Index

Brazil 4, 5, 17, 18, 20, 22, 23, 24, 25, 26, 27, 30
Buffon, Gianluigi 25

Chastain, Brandi 20

FIFA 4, 5, 6, 14, 16, 20, 24, 25, 28, 29, 30

goalkeeper 5, 8, 10, 13, 25

Italy 4, 16, 17, 19, 22, 23, 24, 25, 26, 27, 28, 29

Jules Rimet Cup 5, 29

Pelé 23, 24

Rimet, Jules 5, 7, 28
Ronaldo 22, 23, 30

Salenko, Oleg 23, 27
South Africa 4, 7, 16, 17, 19, 28, 30

Tarpley, Lindsay 25

United States 15, 17, 18, 20, 21, 25, 26, 27, 28
Uruguay 4, 6, 22, 29, 30

Women's World Cup 20, 21, 30
World Cup Trophy 5, 24, 30

Zidane, Zinedine 24

CONTENTS

4 What is the World Cup?

6 World Cup History

8 Laws of the Game

10 The Soccer Pitch

12 Soccer Equipment

14 Qualifying to Play

16 Where They Play

18 Mapping the World Cup

20 Women's World Cup

22 Historical Highlights

24 Legends and Current Stars

26 Famous Firsts

28 The Rise of the World Cup

30 Test Your Knowledge

31 Further Research

32 Glossary/Index

What is the World Cup?

The World Cup of soccer is an international competition. It is played by the best male soccer players in the world. Each country chooses its best players to compete in the event. The **tournament** is organized by the Federation Internationale de Football Association (FIFA). This is the official worldwide group that governs the sport of soccer.

The World Cup takes place every four years. In 2006, 32 countries played in the event. The first World Cup of Soccer took place in Uruguay in 1930. Since then, there have been 17 World Cup competitions.

In 2006, Germany hosted the World Cup for the second time. Italy won the tournament. It was their fourth World Cup win. Only six other countries have won the World Cup. Brazil has won five times, and Germany has won three times. Argentina and Uruguay have both won twice. Great Britain and France have each won the tournament once.

Today, the World Cup is often called the biggest sporting event on Earth. Millions of people attend the games in the country where the tournament takes place. Billions watch World Cup soccer on television.

Fabio Cannavaro was a member of the Italian team that won the 2006 World Cup. Italy defeated France to win its fourth World Cup championship.

In 2010, South Africa will host the world's top soccer teams for the first time. France, Germany, Italy, and Mexico have all hosted the event twice.

CHANGES THROUGHOUT THE YEARS	
PAST	**PRESENT**
The ball was made of hard, painted leather that was sewn with laces.	The ball is made of lightweight, waterproof, synthetic leather.
Thirteen teams played in the World Cup.	Thirty-two teams play in the World Cup.
Soccer was played without official rules.	There are 17 rules, called Laws of the Game.
Players often wore caps or top hats.	Only the goalkeeper is allowed to wear headgear.

The World Cup Trophy

The World Cup Trophy was once called the Victory Cup. In 1946, it was renamed the Jules Rimet Cup. Jules Rimet was the president of FIFA. The original trophy was given to Brazil to keep in 1970. It was the first country to win the World Cup three times. In 1974, a new trophy was made. The winning country keeps it until the next World Cup. It is then given a gold-plated replica.

The World Cup Trophy is made of solid 18-carat gold and weighs 11 pounds (4.9 kilograms). There is enough room on the trophy base to list the world champions until the year 2038.

World Cup History

A disagreement between the International Olympic Committee (IOC) and the soccer organization FIFA led to the first World Cup tournament. FIFA wanted professional soccer players to play in the Olympics. The Olympic committee ruled that only amateur players could compete. FIFA withdrew from the 1932 Olympics. This meant the best players in the world would not be playing in the Olympics. The IOC decided that soccer would not be played at the 1932 Games. Since there was no longer an international soccer competition, FIFA made plans to hold a World Cup tournament.

Cafu was the captain of the Brazil team that won the World Cup in 2002.

The first World Cup took place in Uruguay in 1930. Uruguay had won the Olympic gold medal in 1928. FIFA recognized the country as the world champion. It was given the honor of hosting the first event. Three more World Cup events were held before **World War II** caused a 12-year stop in play.

More than 93,000 fans watched the first World Cup final between Uruguay and Argentina. The Uruguay team won with a score of 4–2.

The competition resumed in 1950. Since then, the World Cup has become one of the world's most popular sporting events. In 1998, about 37 billion people watched the World Cup on television. More than one billion watched the final. Another three million people attended the 64 games that were played during this tournament.

Since 1958, the World Cup has mostly been played in Europe and the Americas. In 2002, the World Cup was played in Asia for the first time. Japan and South Korea co-hosted the event. In 2010, the World Cup will be played in Africa for the first time. South Africa will host the 19th World Cup. The 2014 World Cup tournament will be played on the continent of South America.

Jules Rimet (left) was the president of the French Football Federation from 1919 to 1945.

World Cup Mascots

Like many North American sports, the World Cup has an official mascot. The first official World Cup mascot was a soccer-playing lion named World Cup Willie. He made his appearance at the 1966 event in England. A mascot's costume acts as a symbol for the host country. Mexico's mascot was a jalapeño pepper named Pique. Mexico is known for its spicy food. Nix and Ato were two of the mascots in South Korea. The characters were computer-generated. They represented South Korea's growth in computer graphics and design.

Laws of the Game

Soccer rules are called the Laws of the Game. These rules have not changed much over time. There are 17 Laws of the Game. These are the most common rules.

1 No hands

The only player that can touch the ball is the goalkeeper. The ball cannot touch the body from the fingertips to the shoulders.

2 Offside

An offside is called when a player passes the ball to a teammate. The teammate who receives the pass must not be ahead of the ball when the pass is made. An offside can only occur in the area of the field where goals can be scored.

3 Corner kicks and goal kicks

If the ball goes over the **end line**, a corner kick or a goal kick is called. If the attacking team puts the ball out, the goalkeeper puts it back in play. This is a goal kick. If the defending team puts it out, the other team puts it in play from a corner of the field. This is a corner kick.

4 Direct and indirect free kicks

If a foul is called because of a **hand ball**, a direct free kick is awarded to the attacking team. This means a player can kick the ball directly at the goal. If the referee calls for an indirect free kick, the kicker must pass the ball to a teammate before a shot on goal can be taken.

5 Fouls

A foul is called when one player runs into, trips, pushes, holds, or kicks another player. Only the referee can call a foul.

6 Throw-ins

When the ball is kicked over the **side line** by one team, the other team puts the ball back in play with a throw-in. A player must stand with both feet on the ground and throw the ball over his or her head.

7 Yellow Card and Red Card

A player who commits a serious foul is shown a red card by the referee. That player must leave the game. A player who commits a minor foul is shown a yellow card. That player is warned not to commit another foul. A player shown two yellow cards in one game must leave the game.

Making the Call

Officials in charge of a World Cup game include a referee and two assistant referees. Referees make sure all rules are followed during a game. They keep the official time, call penalties, and hand out yellow and red cards. Assistant referees signal when the ball is out of play. They call offsides, throw-ins, corner kicks, and goal kicks.

The Soccer Pitch

World Cup soccer is played on a rectangular field called a pitch. It is 80 yards (75 meters) wide and 120 yards (110 m) long. The soccer pitch on most professional fields is covered with natural grass. The field is divided into an attacking zone and a defensive zone. The team that is trying to score is the attacking team. The team that is trying to stop a goal from being scored is the defensive team. On each side of the field are side or touch lines. Players who touch the line are out of bounds. The center of the field is marked with a circle. This is where the game begins.

The end of the field is marked by lines called goal lines. If the attacking team hits the ball over the goal line, the defending team gets control of the ball. If the defending team knocks the ball over the end line, the attacking team is awarded a corner kick. In each corner of the field is the corner kick area. A flag is placed there to mark the spot. Corner kicks are taken from here.

There is a goal at each end of the field. The goal is 24 feet (7.3 m) wide and 8 feet (2.4 m) high. Players try to kick the ball into the opposing team's goal. In front of each goal is a box called the penalty area. If an attacking player is fouled in the penalty area, a penalty kick is given. The ball is placed on a mark called the penalty spot. It is right in front of the goal. Any player on the team that was fouled can take a free shot at the goal from the penalty spot.

Players on the Team

In World Cup soccer, there are 11 players per team. Each team has one goalkeeper and 10 other players. Players are defenders or fullbacks, midfielders or halfbacks, and forwards or strikers. A defender's job is to not allow the other team to score. Midfielders control the middle of the field. Sometimes they move up into the attacking zone. Forwards score most of the goals for a team. Most teams in World Cup play use four defenders, four midfielders, and two forwards.

THE SOCCER PITCH

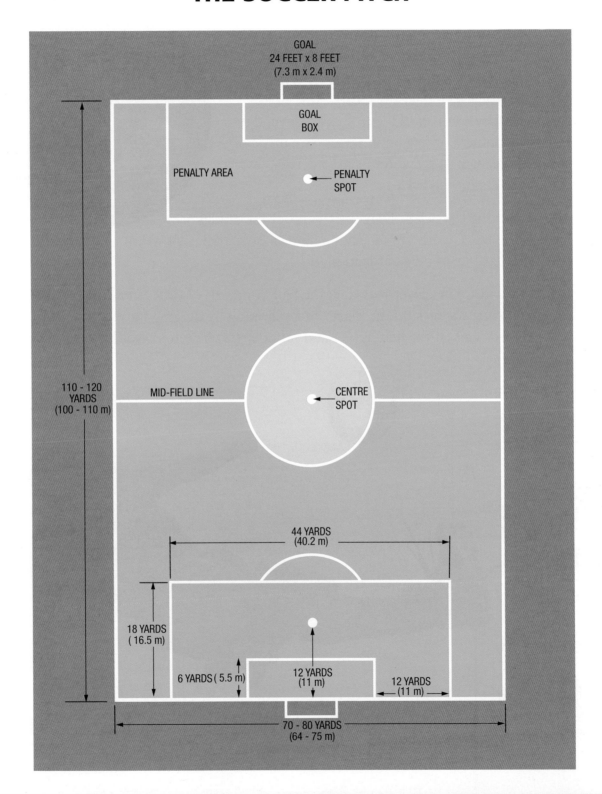

Soccer Equipment

To play soccer, all that is needed is a flat field and a ball. However, most soccer players wear special equipment. They wear a jersey, shorts, shin guards, socks, and soccer shoes. For World Cup soccer players, the jersey often has a emblem or flag on it. Jerseys are made of lightweight material such as polyester or nylon. The player's number and name are on the back.

Shin guards protect the lower leg. They usually cover the ankles and the front of the leg. Guards are made of a hard plastic. Socks are worn over the shin guards to keep the guards in place.

Shoes must be well made. A player may kick the ball hundreds of times in a game. The shoes must have good **cleats**. Cleats stop the player from slipping by digging into the ground. There are different sizes of cleats. If the field is wet and muddy, players often wear longer cleats.

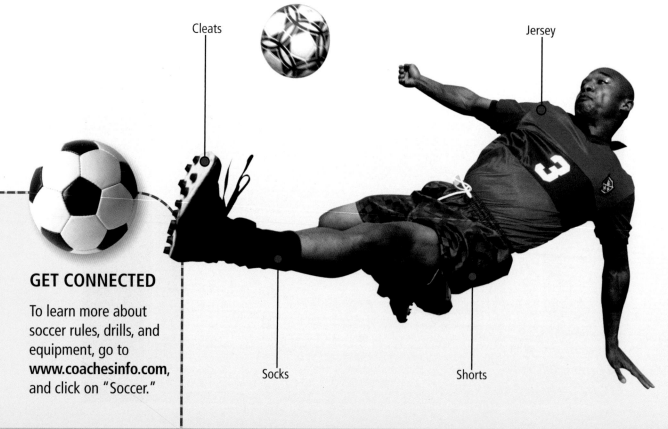

Cleats

Jersey

Socks

Shorts

GET CONNECTED

To learn more about soccer rules, drills, and equipment, go to **www.coachesinfo.com**, and click on "Soccer."

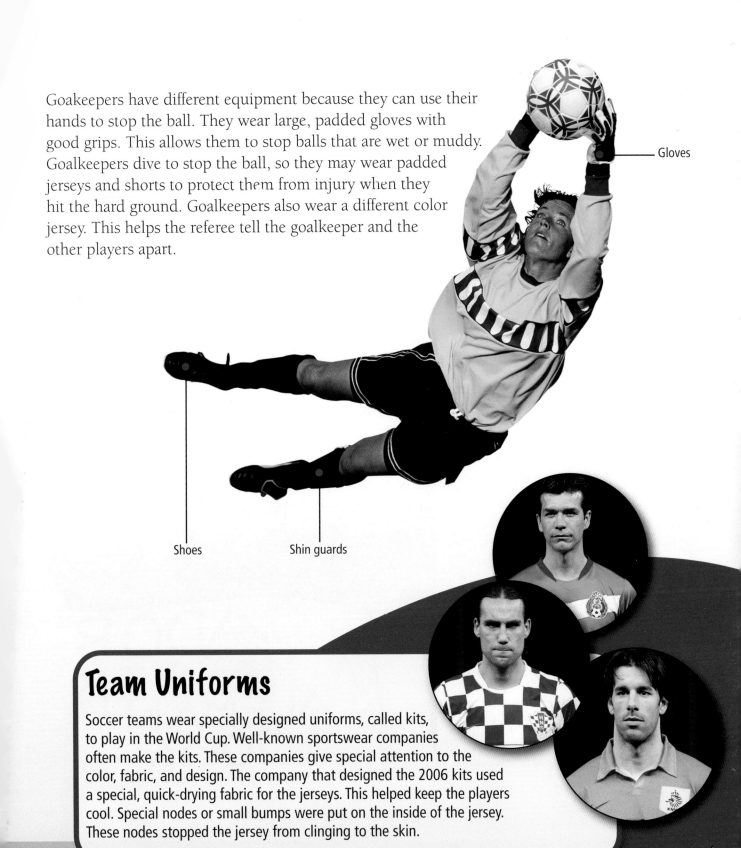

Goakeepers have different equipment because they can use their hands to stop the ball. They wear large, padded gloves with good grips. This allows them to stop balls that are wet or muddy. Goalkeepers dive to stop the ball, so they may wear padded jerseys and shorts to protect them from injury when they hit the hard ground. Goalkeepers also wear a different color jersey. This helps the referee tell the goalkeeper and the other players apart.

Gloves

Shoes

Shin guards

Team Uniforms

Soccer teams wear specially designed uniforms, called kits, to play in the World Cup. Well-known sportswear companies often make the kits. These companies give special attention to the color, fabric, and design. The company that designed the 2006 kits used a special, quick-drying fabric for the jerseys. This helped keep the players cool. Special nodes or small bumps were put on the inside of the jersey. These nodes stopped the jersey from clinging to the skin.

Qualifying to Play

Since 1934, teams have had to earn the right to play in the World Cup. This is known as qualifying. They do this by playing games against other countries in their zone. There are six zones. They are Africa, Asia, Europe, North and Central America and the Caribbean, Oceania, and South America. FIFA decides how many teams from each zone will play in the World Cup. The number is based on the world ranking of the teams in each zone.

Qualifying can start three years before the next World Cup. It takes up to two years to finish. Within each zone, games are played against other countries until the set number of countries remains. Final qualification takes place between September and October of the year before the finals.

The host country is always allowed to play in the World Cup. This is called a **bye**. Until 2006, the defending champions were given a bye. Now, all countries other than the host must compete for a spot in the World Cup. The number of teams allowed to play in the tournament has changed over the years. Since 1998, 32 teams qualify to play in the World Cup.

England made its first appearance at the World Cup in 1950. The team has played in 12 World Cup tournaments. They won the championship when the event was held in England in 1966.

Ecuador made history in 2006 by advancing to the second round of the World Cup for the first time.

In 2006, 198 teams tried to earn a chance to play in the tournament. Germany earned a bye into the tournament. Teams from the six zones tried for the other 31 openings.

The World Cup takes more than a month to play. Teams compete in two stages—the group stage and the knockout stage. During the group stage, eight groups of four teams compete. Each team plays the others in a **round-robin** tournament.

Each group sends its top two teams to the next stage. This is called the knockout stage. During this stage, the winner advances to the next round, and the loser is out of the World Cup. The eight winners of the knockout stage play in a quarter-final round. The four winning teams from this round play in the semi-finals. The two semi-final round winners play for the World Cup.

A special ball was made for each game of the 2006 World Cup tournament. Each ball had the name of the teams that were playing and the date of the game.

CONCACAF

CONCACAF stands for the Confederation of North, Central America and Caribbean Association Football. The United States qualifies for World Cup play by competing in the CONCACAF zone. Teams in CONCACAF zone play each other in a tournament that is held every two years. The winner is awarded the CONCACAF Gold Cup. Forty national associations belong to CONCACAF. Mexico and the United States have played in the most World Cups. Mexico has played in 13 World Cups. The United States has played in eight World Cup tournaments.

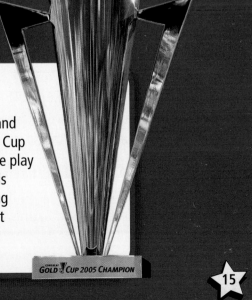

GOLD CUP 2005 CHAMPION

Where They Play

Fireworks lit up the sky after Italy defeated France in the final game of the 2006 World Cup tournament on July 9, 2006.

The host country of the World Cup is chosen by a FIFA executive committee. The committee is made up of members from several different countries. A special voting system is used to decide where the tournament will be held. It is called a transfer vote system. Voting is done in rounds. After each round, the country with the lowest number of votes is eliminated. That eliminated country then transfers, or gives, its votes to the country it would like to see host the event. The voting continues until one country has 51 percent of the vote. That country hosts the World Cup. The voting takes place at least six years before the tournament is held. South Africa received 14 of 24 votes to win the right to play host to the 2010 World Cup.

After the 1958 World Cup, FIFA began to rotate the location of the tournament between Europe and North and South America. This continued until 2002.

In 2002, FIFA introduced a new rule. It decided to rotate the location of the World Cup from zone to zone.

Marcello Lippi coached Italy during the 2006 World Cup. Italy hosted the tournament in 1990.

This means that each zone will have the chance to host the competition every 24 years.

The 2002 World Cup competition was awarded to the Asian zone for the first time. Japan and South Korea were the host countries. This marked the first time that two different countries hosted the same World Cup event. Games were played in ten different cities in each country. The World Cup final was played in Yokohama, Japan.

Ten different cities, including Pretoria, Johannesburg, Cape Town, and Port Elizabeth will host host games during the 2010 World Cup tournament in South Africa.

WORLD CUP WINNERS 1970-2006				
YEAR	HOST	FINAL		
		WINNER	SCORE	RUNNER-UP
1970	Mexico	Brazil	4–1	Italy
1974	West Germany	West Germany	2–1	Holland
1978	Argentina	Argentina	3–1	Holland
1982	Spain	Italy	3–1	West Germany
1986	Mexico	Argentina	3–2	West Germany
1990	Italy	West Germany	1–0	Argentina
1994	United States	Brazil	1–0	Italy
1998	France	France	3–0	Brazil
2002	Japan/Korea	Brazil	2–0	Germany
2006	Germany	Italy	2–1	France

Mapping the World Cup

NORTH
AMERICA

UNITED STATES OF AMERICA – 1984

PACIFIC
OCEAN

ATLANTIC
OCEAN

SOUTH
AMERICA

BRAZIL – 1950

SOUTHERN
OCEAN

The World Cup has been played in 15 countries on five different continents. This map shows when some of those countries have hosted the event.

CONTINENTS THAT HAVE HOSTED THE WORLD CUP

AFRICA – 1 (2010)
ASIA – 1
AUSTRALIA – 0
EUROPE – 10
NORTH AMERICA – 3
SOUTH AMERICA – 4

N
W — E
S

Scale
621 Miles
0   1,000 Kilometers

SPAIN – 1982

JAPAN/KOREA – 2002

EUROPE

ASIA

PACIFIC OCEAN

ITALY – 1934/1990

AFRICA

INDIAN OCEAN

AUSTRALIA

SOUTH AFRICA 2010

SOUTH AFRICA – 2010

Women's World Cup

Until the 1970s, soccer was mostly played by men. Since then, the game has become popular among girls and women. In 1986, FIFA decided to arrange a World Cup event for women.

Like the men's World Cup, the women's tournament is an international tournament. Teams from around the world play qualifying games to earn a place in the competition.

In 1991, the first Women's World Cup championship took place. China was the host country. Twelve teams took part. The United States won the tournament. They defeated Norway by a score of 2–1. The championship drew viewers from around the world. Four years later, Sweden hosted the tournament. Norway won the event with a 2–0 victory over Germany.

In 1999, the United States hosted the 16-country event. The final game was played at the Rose Bowl in Pasadena, California. It was attended by more than 90,000 fans. This is the most people to ever watch a women's sporting event. The United States won a 5–4 **shootout** victory. It was the country's second World Cup win. Brandi Chastain scored the winning goal for the United States. Sissi of Brazil and Sun Wen of China were the leading goal scorers in the competition. They both scored seven goals during the 22 day tournament.

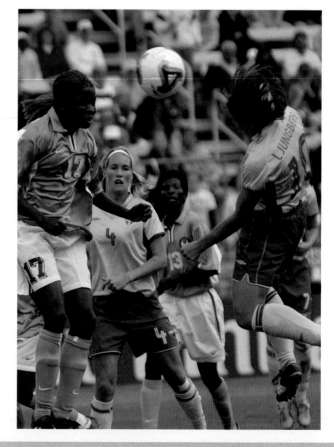

Nigeria and Sweden have played in every Women's World Cup tournament.

GET CONNECTED

Read about the Women's World Cup at **www.fifaworld cup.com**. Click on "FIFA Women's World Cup China 2007."

In 2003, a health crisis in Asia forced the tournament to be held in the United States again. The final game was played at The Home Depot Center in Carson, California. More than 26,000 fans watched Germany defeat Sweden 2–1 to win their first Women's World Cup. Bridgit Prinz of Germany was the top scorer during the tournament. She scored seven goals.

The United States finished the competition in third place. It defeated Canada 3–1 to capture the bronze medal.

In 2007, the Women's World Cup returned to China. Games began in September. Five different cities, including Shanghai and Tiajin, hosted games. Sixteen countries qualified to play in the tournament.

Teams from North and South America, Europe, Africa, and Asia now compete for the top prize in women's soccer.

Aly Wagner has played in more than 100 international soccer games, including the Women's World Cup. She is a member of the United States National Team.

Women's World Cup in the United States

The 1999 Women's World Cup was played in eight stadiums in the United States. Giants Stadium in New Jersey, Soldier Field in Chicago, and Foxboro Stadium in Foxboro, Massachusetts, each hosted games. More than 78,000 fans attended the opening game of the tournament at Giants Stadium. In 2003, games were held in cities such as Boston, Los Angeles, Washington, Portland, and Philadelphia.

Historical Highlights

There have been 18 World Cup tournaments, and hundreds of games have been played. Over the years, the tournament has had numerous historical highlights.

Brazil has won the World Cup a record five times. The country also shares the record for most appearances in the World Cup final with Germany. They have played in the final seven times. Each country has played 92 World Cup games.

In 1950, 174,000 fans watched the game between Uruguay and Brazil. This was the largest crowd to attend a game.

In 1938, 45,000 fans watched Italy and Hungary play in France. This was the smallest crowd to attend a World Cup final game.

Ronaldo Nazario was the top scorer in the 2002 World Cup, with eight goals. He holds the record for most World Cup goals, with 15 goals.

The most goals scored in a World Cup game is 12. Austria defeated Switzerland by a 7-5 score in 1954.

In the 1954 World Cup, Sandor Kocsis of Hungary scored at least two goals in four straight games. He had two goals against Korea, four goals against West Germany, a pair of goals against Brazil, and another two goals against Uruguay.

Brazil's Ronaldo Nazario scored both goals in Brazil's 2–0 win over Germany in the 2002 World Cup final.

The record for the most goals ever scored in one World Cup tournament is held by France's Just Fontaine. He scored 13 goals during the 1958 World Cup in Sweden.

Jair Filho of Brazil, who was better known as Jairzinho, scored in every game he played during the 1970 World Cup event. He finished the tournament with seven goals in six games.

Russia's Oleg Salenko set a World Cup record by scoring five goals against Cameroon during the 1994 World Cup. He tied for the scoring lead, with six goals during the tournament.

Oleg Salenko played in only three World Cup games during his 15-year career. He retired in 2001.

WORLD CUP RECORDS			
RECORD	**PLAYER**	**COUNTRY**	**YEAR(S)**
Most Goals (Career) – 15	Ronaldo Nazario	Brazil	1992
Most Goals (World Cup) – 13	Just Fontaine	France	1958
Most Goals (One Game) – 5	Oleg Salenko	Russia	1994
Most Goals (Cup Final) – 3	Geoff Hurst	England	1966
Most Games Won – 16	Cafu	Brazil	1994–2006
Most Cups Won (Player) – 3	Pelé	Brazil	1958, 1962, 1970
Most Games Played – 25	Lothar Matthäus	Germany	1982–1998
Most Games Coached – 25	Helmut Schön	West Germany	1966–1978
Most Cups Won (Coach) – 2	Vittorio Pozzo	Italy	1934, 1938

LEGENDS
and Current Stars

Zinedine Zidane – Midfielder

Zinedine Zidane was one of France's greatest players. He was known by the nickname Zizou. Zidane first played professional soccer at the age of 17. In 1994, he played on the French national team for the first time. He scored twice against the Czech Republic. A powerful midfielder, Zidane had great speed and **coordination**. In 1998, Zidane helped lead France to the World Cup final. He scored two goals in a 3–0 victory over Brazil. In 1998 and 2002, he was named as the FIFA World Player of the Year. Zidane was injured in the 2002 World Cup, but he returned to play in 2006. He won the Golden Ball Award as the best player in the 2006 World Cup.

Edson Arantes do Nascimento (Pelé)

Pelé – Forward

Edson Arantes do Nascimento is best known as Pelé. He scored 12 goals in World Cup play and helped his Brazilian team win the World Cup Trophy in 1958, 1962, and 1970. Pelé played his first World Cup match in 1958. He scored a goal against Wales in a quarterfinal game. Pelé scored three goals against France in the semi-final. He added two more in the final. In the 1962 World Cup, Pelé scored against Mexico. He was injured in his next game and missed the rest of the event. Pelé played in his third World Cup in 1970. In the final against Italy, he scored three goals. Brazil won the game 4–1. It was the last World Cup game that Pelé would play.

Zinedine Zidane

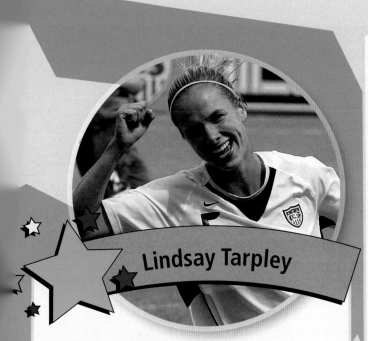

Lindsay Tarpley

Lindsay Tarpley – Midfielder

Lindsay Tarpley is one of the United States' top female soccer players. She helped the United States win gold at the 2004 Olympic Games. In 2002, Tarpley scored the winning goal in the final game of the FIFA U-19 Women's World Championship. This is an international tournament for women under the age of 19. Her goal gave the United States a 1–0 overtime win over Canada. In the 2004 Olympics, Tarpley scored the first goal in the gold medal game. The USA defeated Brazil 2–1. Tarpley started three games for the United States even though she was the second-youngest player on the team.

Gianluigi Buffon – Goalkeeper

Italian goalkeeper Gianluigi Buffon first played top-level soccer when he was 17. He played for the Parma team in Italy's top professional league. Buffon played six years with Parma. He moved on to play with Juventus in 2001. He helped Juventus win the Italian Super Cup in 1999, 2002, and 2003. This is a pre-season tournament that features the top teams in the country. Buffon has been named the FIFA Goalkeeper of the Year three times. He started four games at the 2002 World Cup. At the 2006 World Cup, Buffon did not allow a goal for 453 straight minutes. That is the fifth-longest streak in World Cup history. He let in only one goal during the entire tournament. Buffon was named the top goalkeeper of the 2006 World Cup.

Gianluigi Buffon

Famous Firsts

The first player to score three goals in a game was Guillermo Stabile of Argentina. He did it in Argentina's 6–3 win over Mexico on July 19, 1930.

Vittorio Pozzo was the first man to win two World Cup championships as a head coach. He coached the Italian team to victory in the 1934 and 1938 tournaments.

The first overtime game in the World Cup was played between Austria and France in 1934. Austria won 3–2.

In 1950, the United States beat England 1–0. It was the first time the United States defeated England in World Cup play.

Brazilian player Cafu was the first player to compete in three World Cup finals. He played in the final in 1994, 1998, and 2002.

In 1982, Spain hosted the first 24-team World Cup event. Italy won its third World Cup title. The Italian team defeated Germany 3–1.

Cafu (left) played in his third World Cup final when Brazil defeated Germany in the 2002 championship game.

Oleg Salenko of Russia was the first player to score five goals in a single World Cup game. He did it against Cameroon in the 1994 World Cup.

Brazil became the first team to win four World Cup titles in 1994. In the final, Brazil defeated Italy 3–2.

In 1994, Brazil defeated Italy 3–2 in the first World Cup final decided by penalty kick goals. The teams were tied 0–0 after 90 minutes of regular time. Neither team was able to score in the 30-minute overtime period.

Laurent Blanc of France scored the first **golden goal** in World Cup play. He scored it against Paraguay in 1998.

Brazil is the only country to play in all 18 World Cup events. It has won the World Cup a record five times.

World Cup in the United States

When the United States hosted the World Cup in 1994, games were played across the country. Cities such as Boston, Chicago, Detroit, New York, San Francisco, and Los Angeles hosted games. The total attendance was a record 3,567,415. Millions of fans watched the games on television in the United States.

The United States team were in Group A. They played three games in the opening round. The team tied Switzerland, defeated Columbia, and lost to Romania. The United States advanced to the second round, but lost to Brazil by a 1–0 score.

The Rise of the World Cup

1904

FIFA forms in Paris, France. Soccer groups from France, Belgium, Denmark, the Netherlands, Spain, Sweden, and Switzerland join FIFA. The first FIFA international game is held between Belgium and France. England, which started its Football Association in 1863, did not join.

1905

The Football Association joins FIFA. Later, Austria, Germany, Hungary, Italy, Ireland, Scotland, and Wales join.

1900

Soccer is played at the Olympic Games for the first time. Great Britain wins the gold medal.

1910

South Africa becomes the first non-European country to join FIFA.

1912

Argentina and Chile join FIFA.

1913–1918

The United States joins FIFA. International games are played in countries that are not at war during **World War I**.

1921

Jules Rimet becomes FIFA's third president. When he became president, FIFA had 20 members. When he retired in 1954, 85 countries were members of FIFA.

1924 and 1928

Soccer becomes an official Olympic sport. FIFA organizes the event. Uruguay wins in both years.

1930

The first World Cup is held in Montevideo, Uruguay.

1934

The World Cup final is broadcast on the radio for the first time.

1938

France hosts the World Cup. Italy defeats Hungary 4–2.

1982

Twenty-four countries compete for the World Cup in Spain.

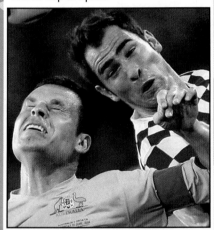

1998

A record thirty-two countries compete at the World Cup in France.

QUICK FACTS

- In 1966, the Jules Rimet Cup was stolen. British police recovered the trophy after a dog named Pickles found it hidden under a hedge.

- More than 200 million people play soccer around the world. FIFA is now one of the largest sports associations in the world.

- Only 300 people attended the Romania and Peru game at the 1930 World Cup.

- India did not attend the 1950 World Cup because its players were not allowed to play barefoot.

Test Your Knowledge

1 Which country has the most World Cup wins?

2 What was the original World Cup Trophy called?

3 Which country hosted the first World Cup?

8 Who has played in three World Cup final games?

9 When did the U.S. host the Women's World Cup?

10 Where was the 2007 Women's World Cup held?

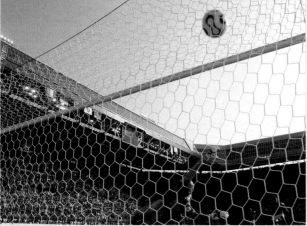

4 Where will the 2010 World Cup take place?

5 What is the size of a World Cup soccer goal?

6 What organization governs soccer?

7 Who has scored the most World Cup goals?

ANSWERS: 1) Brazil **2)** the Victory Cup **3)** Uruguay **4)** South Africa **5)** 24 feet (7.3 m) wide and 8 feet (2.4 m) high **6)** FIFA **7)** Ronaldo of Brazil **8)** Cafu **9)** 1999 and 2003 **10)** China